TRUMP:

A Lesson for America 2020

(Based on Opinion, Research & Media Reporting)

By: Dennel B Tyon

A Middle-ground Ministries Imprint

"I Am the Chosen One"

I didn't think President Trump could surprise me anymore... but on August 21st, 2019, during a press conference, on the Whitehouse lawn, he went and did it! After virtually insulting every *Jewish* person "who chooses to vote Democratic," by saying that they are "extremely disloyal," if they vote that way, and then doubling down on that comment again, when pressed by reporters to clarify, he turned to discussing his efforts to penalize China, by imposing tariffs (which are now actually costing American consumers millions in increased prices), acting as if it was a good thing, despite the harm it causes to individuals, he said, "somebody had to do It."

Then, this man actually turned and looked at the sky, lifting his arms, outreached to the heavens, and proclaimed, "***I am the chosen one.***" I was astounded when I saw this, gasping, 'oh no you didn't...' as I shook my head in disbelief. But I had just witnessed it. It was for real. I had always thought Trump was a complete and total narcissist, but really? He really believes he is "the chosen one"? That just confirmed it for me.

But there might be something to it. He claims to be religious… in fact, "probably *the most religious person in the* world," he would say; though, I don't see a **spiritual** bone in that man's body. He has no love for others – only for himself. It's only okay, if it benefits him, whatever "it" may happen to be… and if anyone else gets hurt in the process, then so be it. The man really thinks HE *IS the chosen one!!* So, what do you think? Is he?

Could this all have been 'meant to be'? I mean, I've always been a believer in "everything happens for a reason," and, this *is* testing **our** faith. In all honesty, I knew in my heart that Trump was going to win the 2016 election; so, I voted for him. For some reason, it seemed, he needed to win that election, and even though I have found myself wondering, at times, if I was right, I felt it was the right thing to do at the time, given the circumstances. Since that is s how I've always tried to make decisions throughout my lifetime, I followed my heart and swallowed the bitter pill of Trump becoming President of the United States.

For whatever reason (and I'm now of the opinion that it was to OPEN OUR EYES), I believed that, at that point in time, Donald John Trump needed to be president. He *has* done some momentous things; I want to be sure to give credit, where credit is due here… and I'm certain I don't know nearly every single thing he has done, that might have done some good for us, and/or for the world, but of what I do know, I will speak.

First and foremost, for me: When he stepped over that line between North and South Korea – that was HUGE! I was taken back to my childhood. This man, whom I grew up to "know" as a cruel, brutal and awful dictator, a frightening and overbearing ruler, whom no one dared cross, or challenge, ***I now SAW reaching out***, shaking the hand of our president, and welcoming him to step over the line… into North Korea; a place *no other* U.S. President has ever stood. This is something of a distinction.

I had to admire him for that; and he seemed to get along with the leaders of Canada, France, and Germany, too, at first, and his chemistry with Russia's President Putin was undeniable. In fact, we have found out now (8-18-2020) that he was actually in contact with Putin several times during the 2016 campaign, apparently encouraging interference through advertising on Facebook and elsewhere, aside from openly requesting their help before reporters (i.e. "Russia, if you're listening…). But that aside, for now, he's also being credited – by some, more than others – for assisting with the peace deals that Isreal has been making with surrounding countries; last year, they signed a peace accord with Egypt, and then a few months later, with Jordan. On August 13, 2020, it was announced that Isreal was signing a new peace deal, the Abraham Accord, named after The Father of the Three Great Faiths, and one of Trump's team proclaimed that Donald should be given the Nobel Peace Prize.

However, there are so many other reasons that I just cannot find it in myself to respect this man much more than that. He is rude and crude and perverted and bigotted and chauvenistic and narcissictic and hateful and he truly is a pathological liar. I find myself on the fence about his claim to be "the chosen One," though. He just might be. Trump has proudly proclaimed that he loves division amongst people. Well, now he has it. There isn't even just us and them anymore – there is us, and them, *and the others.*

The Democratic, & Democratic-Socialist Dream

I never understood the need for classification, but people in general, seem to love it. Can't we just accept each other as PEOPLE? Will there ever be a place and time that we see one another as purely human? Or, even better... as *spiritual* beings, having this mysterious human experience together. There are others who feel the way I do... I know that now. I am not alone. It's no wonder I feel for "the others."

I've been one of the 'others' all of my life, never belonging to 'us' or 'them.' The only kids in school I dared talk to were the underdogs; the ones nobody else talked to... and "Others" just always seemed drawn to me, two-legged and four. Animals are people to me; just little souls, having an animal experience. I talk to the grass, the trees, the birds, the insects – you name it, I've probably talked it once or twice in my lifetime. With or without any other soul around, I will conversate, because I know *somebody* is listening.

Joe will do just fine, if he gets elected; anyone is better than four more years of Trump. Bernie would have just made a lot of changes that I would, personally, like to see made to our government (you know, structure and operations...).

Something more akin to my childhood *Utopian dream,* which I still plan to achieve (despite my mother's negative influence).

In my dreams, I see a vast amount of acreage with a small community, surrounding a Mental Health Fitness and Spiritual Wellness Center, and Animal Sanctuary, powered by green energy (wind, geo-thermal and solar), hopefully generating so much power that we'll receive a check from the electric company every month instead of a bill. A closed community, but with the Center open to the public for a price... possibly some little stores up front; laundromat, feed store, plant nursery, whatnot. But whatever the future holds, the one thing I know is *we just can't survive four more years of Trump.*

PERSONALITY: An Issue Itself

On August 25th, last year (2019), Republican Joe Walsh gave an interview with George Stephanopoulos, announcing his plan to run against Trump in the primaries as a potential Republican presidential nominee. He said our current president Is "nuts, erratic, cruel" and "incompetent" and has "no freaking clue what he is doing," and he calls him "a narcissist." He says one good thing Trump has done, is make him "reflect" on some of the things *he* has said or done and *apologize* for any ugly politics of his own in the past. He said he feels responsible for having helped "create Trump." Ultimately, he says Trump is "not capable of being decent; he's cruel [and] bigoted."

I'm not sure where he went; never heard much more from him, but it appears no one is running against Trump, now, except Joe Biden. Joe Walsh refers to Trump being "a child in the Whitehouse"! **Kudos**, Joe. See my book, The Child President. He says, Trump "has already tweeted us into a recession," and fears "he'll tweet us into war."

In another interview, this same day, Trump was asked if he had any second thoughts about anything. He replied, "I have second thoughts about everything." Lol. I find that hilarious. He's always contradicting himself, changing his mind, speaking out both sides of his mouth, and hiring and firing people with differing opinions of each one at each point in time.

On August 30, 2019, a writer for The New Yorker told Chris Hayes, Trump "has a sort of malignant charisma about him" and said, there is "insanity in his rhetoric." A congressman from California said, "we have a sociopath in the Whitehouse;" and Psychology Today wrote an article about all of the narcissistic traits Trump possess; lying, exaggerating, boasting, demeaning others, etc. I did a school Psychology paper on that exact subject: A Doctoral Student's Psychological Analysis of America's Current President. Got an "A" – (smiling).

Further, Trump has filed hundreds of individual lawsuits against people, over the years, in an effort to "hide behind the law" (MSNBC, 3-3-2020). He has only continued this pattern, while in office, filing suits against every single person who has been "harassing" him to see his taxes, or anyone he has screwed – literally, or figuratively. Lord help anyone who dares break a Non-Disclosure Agreement *that he forced them to sign.* Always claiming they are just "retaliating against him," because of his political views," or whatever, Trump lies through his teeth and continues to hide his past tax returns. Never mind the fact that most presidents willingly release their taxes upon election.

What Do World Leaders and Others Think of Trump?

When Trump discussed the idea of purchasing the country of Greenland, last year, being turned down by its Prime Minister, who told him "Greenland is not for sale," calling his idea "absurd," Trump said that he felt her response was "nasty." I'm sure she has absolutely no respect for him. On August 23, 2019, Trump escalated the trade war with China, which he, personally, created the month prior; tacking on an additional 30% tariff, after China increased prices on goods to America, in response to his original tariffs. The Dow dropped and the *market* panicked… people were talking recession because of his careless actions; analysists say that he "thrives on chaos."

Last year, The Prime Minister of Britain called him a "buffoon," likely more than once. Others have compared him to a "rodeo clown" and many called him a "trust-fund baby." He has also been likened to "a mob boss" and a "cult leader," by witnesses under oath. So much has happened in this past year, and Trump has been almost absent through it all; doing absolutely nothing, really, when there was much to be done.

Additionally, financial records have been uncovered, proving that he *has* lied on paperwork for loans, for taxes, and for expenses from his various companies (which he was supposed to have nothing to do with once he became president). On August 10th 2020, reporter, Don Lemon said, straight up, "the president of the United States is a fraud and a conman." Rand Paul called him an Orange Windbag;

SCHEMES, BRIBES & POSSIBLE TAX FRAUD

Attorney General, Letitia James, in an interview with Rachael Maddow, on August 23, 2019, said that everything Trump has ever done is now being investigated, adding, **"no one *is above the law,* not even the President of these United States."** She added that they are looking into the taxes of the NRA, too; they had sued her office because she wanted to depose Oliver North, regarding the NRA's financial dealings. They claimed a violation of attorney-client privilege but lost.

The Attorney General will be interviewing Oliver North shortly, and "looking into the NRA" *and* "individuals who contributed to [it]." Current and past board members, are now cooperating with the investigation. UPDATE 8-10-2020: The New York Attorney General has filed a complaint with eighteen counts (charges) of fraud and illegal transfers of money against the founder and four members of the board of the NRA; she is asking for the complete and total dissolution of the 150 year old organization. He, sharing with them so they didn't tell, spent the money on personal purchases and extravagent trips and parties on a 100-foot yacht!

In months still to come, in the Supreme Court, there will be an argument session about Trump's taxes and financial records, which he has been fighting the exposure of, since prior to the election, up to now. Rachael Maddow calls his reaction "hyper-desperation" to stop these records from becoming public; legal battle after legal battle. She supposes he might even refuse the orders of the Supreme Court, if they were to rule against him; however, she points out that it would actually be his overseas bank, Deutsche Bank, which would need to respond to those orders.

*UPDATE: On July 9th 2020, the Supreme Court ruled

against Trump's claim, saying, he is not above the "common duty to produce evidence when called upon in a court proceeding." He will have to release his taxes and financial paperwork after all. UPDATE 8-10-2020: It has been announced that Trump's personal bank, in Germany, was subpoenaed last year and has already long-complied with the subpoena, turning over every financial record they had on Donald J. Trump within months of the order.

Trump's niece, Mary (the daughter of the sister, mentioned above), is now finishing the writing of her own book, entitled Too Much and Never Enough: How my Family Created the World's most Dangerous Man. Early excerpts of this publication tell of Schemes that involved the entire family, led by their father Fred, of course; she says that Donald did his best to make his father happy, by becoming like him as much as possible; " lying… became a way to survive" for her Uncle, she says. UPDATE: 8-10-2020: The book has been released and there is a lot of information in there that explains why Trump is, the way he is.

Trump University was a "scheme" from the very start; he was ordered to pay twenty-five million dollars, cash, to the victims of this scheme; then there was the Miss America pageant, which he bought and then sold, and the charity, where he raised money, and pledged a million dollars *of his own money*, for veterans, then bought a 6-foot tall portrait of himself with some of the money, and used of it $258,000.00 to "settle legal problems." Hush money payments to Stormy Daniels were claimed as "legal expenses," on his tax return, as disclosed by a small portion of the records discovered. The New York Times has put together a forty-page expose' about the president and his siblings running many different schemes in order to evade taxes, ripping off the city, the government, their tenants, (showing over one billion dollars in business losses). In fact, his sister, Maryanne, was given a lifetime seat on the federal judiciary, in order to avoid an impending ethics inquiry into her role in an illegal tax scheme, which she conducted with her brother, Donald John Trump. His inauguration in 2017, itself, is being investigated for fraud... the administration claimed it cost more than Obama's 2009 inauguration, which was the largest in U.S. history. But the numbers don't add up. Rick Gates has already admitted that "it's possible" he stole from that inauguration.

The rule of law has been perverted to serve the president,

rather than to serve justice; he is the first president since Nixon, not to turn over his taxes. The IRS admitted months ago that Trump had lied on his IRS tax returns for a golf resort he owns in Scotland; and he lied on his Scottish tax report too. He has made one excuse after another as to why he is not able to turn ANY of these records over. It was, also, recently discovered that there were "some inappropriate efforts to mishandle Trump's audit" as well. Hmmm. Could it possibly be that somebody tried to influence the auditor's decision with a bribe???

SHOOTINGS & Terroristic Violence:

A symptom of Trump?

1. In Charlottesville, VA, 2019, Trump encouraged the hateful speech of white supremist and insisted that there were "fine people on both sides."

2. There have been some thwarted, planned mass shootings (three on 8-22-19); altogether… 14 would-be shooters have been arrested since the El Paso and Dayton shootings, due to people reporting suspicions (having been encouraged by

3. police to 'see something; say something' if, and when, they have concerns about a relative or coworker, or see anything suspicious). On August 23rd, a massive plot was stopped when they uncovered a shitload of automatic weapons at a Marriot Hotel. An ex-employee was planning to shoot the place up any day. Certainly, this increase in violence is due to the rhetoric and hatred, which has been spewed by our current President for years now.

4. Trump is claiming mental health issues are the problem. He actually said, "mental health pulls the trigger, not people." Yet, Trump appears to suffer from MANY mental health issues himself, which he obviously doesn't recognize... this is just one of many statements he has made, not only in the past, but in the recent weeks, blaming everything, except our current gun laws, for the increased violence.

5. He has also blamed "immigrants" for the violence, in general, as if numbers are even close in comparison to violent acts committed by U.S.-born citizens. They are not, by the way.

IMMIGRANTS: America's Foundation

Even though Trump's parents were immigrants, only coming to this country after the Civil War, Trump seems to think no one else should have a right to migrate here anymore. He seems to fail to remember that this great country was originally built by the sweat and labor of immigrants; in fact, every single one of us, apart from Native Americans, are either descendants of immigrants, if not immigrants, ourselves... or are descendants of slaves brought in by immigrants, who thought they were better than everyone else because of their white skin.

We should be proud of the fact that we are a land of immigrants and of the fact that we finally realized skin color **doesn't** make anyone any better than anyone else. We should be welcoming of *others*, so long as they have good intentions. A simple, psychological evaluation would weed out any truly dangerous immigrants. We could develop a way to deal with these particular people, rather than just locking everybody up, as they cross the border, like we still seem to be doing now.

Children are being taken from their parents – and have been, for over two years now - for no reason other than to punish the *parents* for trying to come here to give their children a better life; many are STILL being held in detention centers, no better than concentration camps, if even nearly as good! What, exactly, did these poor children do to deserve being locked up like criminals? First, being separated from parents at the border, with no particular cause, except that Trump ordered it to be done. Now caged, with no idea why, they are getting sick and dying.

How awful a country we have become in this manner since the election of Donald John Trump. We, the people… once claiming that we believed all *men* were created equal, now treat *"others"* worse than we treat most animals. I don't understand that.

Downplaying Science & Severity

Now we have a life and death situation, which Trump is doing his best to minimalize; the newest Coronavirus, *Covid-19*. Trump was talking about "the numbers," as he was being interviewed, regarding whether or not another cruise ship with a thousand, or so, more Americans onboard, should be left quarantined at sea, or allowed to dock in Florida. He said he "would like the numbers to stay where they are" and if we allowed this ship to be brought back to America, "then obviously, the numbers would go up." The "240 currently sick, and the 24...," (he says) are now dead from this virus, "would go up." There was no mention of any feeling for these individual people; they are just numbers to him.

As of *March 3, 2020*, the count, according to the John Hopkins Center for Systems, Science & Engineering, supported by the Centers for Disease Control, is more than **100,000** cases of Covid-19 **(worldwide),** which has turned fatal for more than **3,400** people around the world. In the United States, alone, we had confirmed **335** people sick at the time, of which, **17;** fourteen in Washington state, one in California, and two in Florida, *were now dead.* This number is only going to up from here, for the next year, to a year and a half, according to the CDC, as that is how long it will take to get "any meaningful reduction from a vaccine. It takes at least a year to perform all of the trials, scientists say.

By March 6, 2020, the number in the U.S. went up to **400+,** by March 7th to **450;** the morning of March 8th, it was

475, and by evening, it was **490**. Rising quickly. More than **500** just after midnight; **1000+** three days later and **300** more in the next twenty-four hours. A week later, March 15, 2020, with numbers still rising, there are **2,955 infected** and **60 dead, in the United States...** as well as, *153,400 known sick* and *over 3,300 dead, worldwide.*

A month later, there were over **39,000 American lives claimed** by Covid19 and **730,000+** known cases in the US. Worldwide, the count had reached **2,214,861** known ill and **150,948** deaths. *Less* than *another* month later, one person was dying every 32 seconds! As of the end of August, confirmed cases are in the **millions...** and known deaths have reached *hundreds of thousands*, worldwide AND in America.

Trump accuses the Democrats of "politicizing the Coronavirus," saying the numbers given for deaths (3.4%), by the officials, "is really a false number," readily admitting, however, that "it is just a hunch." Then he compared the test kits available at that time, to his phone call with the Ukrainian President, saying they "are all perfect, *like the letter.*"

Staunch supporters of Trump, interviewed by MSNBC, say, they believe Trump; they do not think the virus exists. "It's all a hoax," says one lady, being interviewed by an MSNBC reporter. Regarding the numbers provided by the CDC, she says, "I don't believe them at all." So, is this woman taking ANY PRECAUTIONS against this new virus now sweeping the world? I'm sure not; and thereby, she is endangering every single person she comes in contact with… and she is only one of the many "forever-Trumpers."

It's All About the "Numbers"

Does trump really believe "keeping the numbers low" (as far as reporting to the public) does anyone any good? If we aren't honest about how and where this virus is spreading, we are going to have an even worse problem… and it is spreading quick! Hiding the fact, doesn't change the fact. The rest of the world is taking immense precautions, in every single aspect; mass gatherings have been outlawed, professional sports games are being played in empty stadiums all over, and models strutted the walkway in front of an imaginary audience at popular fashion shows in Italy.

Concerts have been cancelled all over (even Texas cancelled their annual South x Southwest concert this summer) This is no joke people.

Pence hesitates to provide any information on test kits, when pressed by Jake Tapper for answer as to how many people in America have been tested, and are being tested, or will be tested; he said, assuring everyone on Trump's behalf, that we "could expect millions to be tested within weeks." It did not happen. It's really hard to believe any statement from this administration anymore... after all, Trump has been lying to us from the start.

THE ECONOMY: Over A Decade of Improvement

Trump's one righteous claim, being the economy, may not even be a valid one, for more than one reason. First, being, that the economy has actually been on a TWELVE-YEAR upward swing (since the Obama years). Trump did not cause the rise; he just, hasn't caused it to drop, yet. He started the trade war on purpose, saying "someone had to take on China" (when proclaiming himself "the chosen one," in the Rose Garden). It is estimated that this trade war will cost every American approximately $1,000.00 a year.

Those tax cuts he bragged about signing into law last year, only benefited the wealthy... and large corporations. He said the benefit would "trickle down." It hasn't yet, nor do I believe it will. He claims a victory of low unemployment, yet more people lost their jobs last year than ever before; many likely found new ones, just before the unemployment count.

Now, with the Covid19 pandemic, the market is struggling; it made its first upward movement in a week just after the first Super Tuesday vote this year... a sign that people still have hope that, with a new president, we can fix the mess Trump has gotten us in. But only a few stocks are moving up; overall the market is still unstable.

A House IMPEACHMENT, Well Deserved

The Ukraine scandal is what ultimately led to Trump's impeachment, although six separate investigations were actually being conducted under the "formal umbrella" of Impeachment, as Nancy Pelosi stated; and I watched every minute of the House proceedings that I was able. Several Whitehouse staffers were deposed by our Representatives, since the House feels leaders of the Department of Justice can no longer be trusted to tell the truth.

By October 16, 2019, the Impeachment inquiry is three weeks in… Things weren't looking good for trump. Criminal referrals have been made against the president, more than once, in the past two years. The Attorney General, William Barr, has simply refused to investigate any of them. This might lead to a LOT of people getting in trouble down the road.

There is ample evidence of actual crimes, and the attempt to cover them up (i.e. putting paperwork in a "super-secret server,"); and there is even further impeachable offenses: *four* people were indicted, who were associated with Rudy Gulliani, Trump's "personal" lawyer, who has been taking government trips *to visit with foreign leaders,* still looking for dirt on Trump's most likely opponent, Joe Biden, and his son. Additionally, Gulliani appears to be part of a "counter-intelligence investigation," somehow, which is just frightening to think.

Ukraine appears to be bending to Trump's pressure, as Ukrainian security officers, since, have targeted Hunter Biden in a

New Dossier. Another federal grand jury subpoena was issued, more charges are expected, and new indictments are possible. Paul Manafort, the guy who wrote the Dossier, is already in federal prison, for tax evasion, and now two men, associated with Ukrainian billionaire, Dmitry Firtash, the man who financed all of their dealings in that area, are also on their way to prison. Firtash was a Putin ally, installed there, as a player in the energy business, and linked to Russian organized crime.

By December 2019, the House hearings had become enthralling, or at least, I thought so. My nephew got annoyed that that's all I had on at times, but I found the whole process fascinating; and, I learned so much information! God bless Nancy Pelosi. She did everything within her power to try to see this all the way through, as justly as possible.

I was impressed with the whole process (at least, in the House). It was formal, civilized and extremely serious in tone. Seventeen witnesses in all, ended up coming forward, despite Trump's orders to ignore all subpoenas. Bless them all. The testimony was damning, all put together; Sondland's, alone, seemed like enough to take Trump out of office, and yet, what did *he* get in return? Retribution, eventually.

Ambassador Yovanavich was most impressive… and in the midst of her testimony, while being broadcast live, Trump was tweeting what seemed to be threatening remarks about,

and directly to, Ambassador Yovanavich! The House Chair informed her about the tweets while she was on the stand and asked what she thought about it. She said it seemed that it was intended to be threatening, and that it did, indeed, make her feel threatened a little bit. But Alexander Vindman, most of all, was the one witness I ADMIRED, as he read a letter to his deceased father, thanking him for bringing him to America, "where truth matters," and promised his father than he "would be okay for telling the truth…". At least, he wouldn't be killed for it. The retaliation he received from this vindictive president, however, was despicable – not to mention, his twin brother, being removed, obviously, just out of spite.

True Justice Denied

Despite all of the evidence gathered by the House, and testimony shown to the Senate, *via video recordings*, the Republican-majority Senate, ultimately voted to find this president *"not guilty"* of the Impeachment charges, despite the fact that many of them admitted, openly, that what Trump had done was wrong; and many more said so in secret. Many may now be regretting their decision.

O*nly one* Republican senator, **Utah's Mitt Romney**, was brave enough, and *devoted to his belief in god, to such an extent,* **that he could not vote against his conscience,** after having taken that sacred oath. **I'm in awe of his strength and conviction;** and so PROUD of him, (Utah, being my extended-family's home-state).

The 'not guilty' vote, however, does NOT UNDO the impeachment, itself. Trump *will* forever be known as the third president in U.S. history to be IMPEACHED. He was impeached, *two-fold*, in fact, and remains, impeached, as Speaker Pelosi said, **"forever."**

After the Fact

So many more things have been discovered, that in themselves should be impeachable, since the so-called "impeachment trial," which was truly just a joke in the end, it is just ridiculous. Nice that they went through all the formality, though. It was interesting to see how it is all *supposed to be done*. But, really, the Senate Trial was all for show – so that the Republicans could say they followed procedure (to some extent). I don't understand how they can rationalize setting a new precedent, like this, for trying of impeachments, without the requirement of witnesses being heard or evidence being submitted in the Senate. This becomes a very slippery slope now. Any incoming president in the future (including Trump, if, God forbid, our electoral representatives vote him in again) can feel free to commit any offenses they wish, for their own personal benefit, and know that they will face no penalty whatsoever.

What kind of a democracy, or republic, *or society* for that matter, *does that leave us with?* The Federal Judges Association called an "emergency meeting" February 18, 2020, for what was being referred to as a "rule of law crisis"...that, being, Attorney General William Barr intervening in "multiple, active federal criminal cases, going as far back as the beginning of his tenure, apparently giving "preferential treatment to friends of the president."

This, only just bursting into view because of Barr's latest demands for a more lenient sentence for Roger Stone, another good friend of the president. He was sentenced to three and a half years; Trump commuted that sentence June 10, 2020, one day before the sentence was to begin.

More than two thousand *federal* judges have come out, now, to say they believe Attorney General Barr should resign, or be impeached, at this point. It has been determined that he has "gone above and beyond to undermine the constitution – and the truth – to protect Donald Trump", in that he, in fact, lied about the Mueller Report in more than one way.

He "parroted Russian disinformation campaigns," attacked the integrity of various law enforcement agents, inside of his own department, and let Trump's friends 'off the hook' after conviction, by intervening in cases at the Department of Justice, having any "conflict with Trump's personal interests." Above all, we are told, Bill Barr was found to be involved in creating the "clearinghouse for Rudy Guliani to hand over manufactured dirt on" one or more political opponents of Trump (Racheal Maddow, MSNBC, Feb. 2020). So, *how did we get here ??*

In The Beginning

There was "the email scandal," for which Trump pointed the finger at Hillary Clinton, for reasons which are still not completely clear to me. This is where he called for Russia to "investigate" Hillary's emails. He was being investigated at that time, for several other things, including the tax fraud and accusations of sexual harassment (e.i. Stormy Daniels, etc.), but chose to deflect and project his own guilt upon others. All the claims against Hillary turned out to be nothing. Many claims against Trump, on the other hand, were verified, and some are still pending action.

He said he had to "drain the swamp," but he never fully explained what he meant by that. If he drained anything at all, it seems, he drained the most vital agencies and most knowledgeable parts of our government, and of the Whitehouse Staff. From what I hear, he has no more than a skeleton crew running the operations inside the Whitehouse, and most positions are held by "actors." Trump says he likes it that way (admitting that's because 'acting' personnel do not have to be vetted).

Then there was the "Russian collusion scandal..." a "hoax," according to our great president; "a complete, a total, hoax," which has been completely investigated, verified, and compiled in a very thick report, prepared by the head of the Department of Justice, at the time, Robert Mueller. Direct evidence of numerous crimes committed by the president, and his associates, was found. Evidence of direct communications between Trump and Russia's president, Vladimir Putin, was also found, specifically, regarding Trump's apparent desire to build a new 'Trump Hotel,' in Russia! But Trump also dismissed all of this as "a hoax."

Recently, it has been found that Russia had put bounties on the lives of our soldiers in Afghanistan. Trump claimed to know nothing about it; he says he wasn't ever told. Evidence *has come to light that proves Trump was briefed, at least twice...* last year and this February, that Russians were paying bounties for dead American soldiers. Professor J. Cobb says, "the idea that the president *not reading* something, is an excuse" for not knowing, is ridiculous.

Attorney General Barr twisted the facts in the Mueller Report, attempting to make it seem as though nothing was found to have been done wrong, proving again and again he is not in it to help the American people. He's in it to protect Trump at all costs. Yet, he complains how all of Trump's tweets are making it "impossible" for him to do his job. Trump tells a reporter, with absolutely no concern, that he "agrees" that his tweets *are* "probably making [Barr's] job harder," which is why, he says, he "made the decision NOT TO intervene" (but intervening is exactly what he did)… it was then that Trump actually proclaimed himself "Chief Law Enforcement Officer."

Next came the Ukraine scandal. That "perfect phone call," as it was described by Trump at the time, which actually launched the formal impeachment investigation by the House of Representatives. Once again, Trump says he did "nothing wrong." However, on October 3rd 2019; Trump said, right before reporters, that he "hoped Ukraine would look into it…" because he felt it was important to know if Joe had done anything illegal.

Really, all he was trying to do was to dig up dirt on Joe Biden, *if at all possible*, by "looking into" a position held by Biden's son, Hunter, at a Ukrainian-owned oil company. It was found that he was on the Board of Directors. Trump questioned the amount of money he was being paid, what he actually did for them, (if anything at all) and questioned Hunter's qualification for the job (which makes me laugh, when I think about the irony there). Trump asserted that Hunter only got the position because he was Joe Biden's son, and insinuated that, somehow, it benefited Joe. I think that was the jest of it. It never panned out anything, though, because there wasn't any dirt to be found.

The common belief, understanding and reporting of the media, is that Trump felt Joe Biden was going to be his most likely competitor in the upcoming election (and he was correct, it seems). He thought if he could make it look like Biden had done something sneaky, maybe people wouldn't vote for him. So, in a nutshell, what Trump was attempting to do was to force the Ukrainian president – by *extorting* him – into submitting to Trump's desire for an investigation to be "announced," against Joe and Hunter Biden, whether or not it was actually followed through with. Just the announcement, itself, in particular, seemed important to Trump.

The irony is, what Trump was trying to stop from happening, is exactly what *is* happening now. Out of a beginning field of twenty, extremely diverse, potential candidates, it came down to Bernie Sanders and Joe Biden; seeing Reverend Jessie Jackson endorse Bernie Sanders, for the Democratic candidate for President (March 8, 2020), gave me hope but Bernie conceded to support Joe not long after. All of the other candidates, one-by-one, also conceded to Joe Biden for the Democratic nomination.

Since his so-called acquittal, this president has proclaimed himself the "chief law enforcement officer"... (or, in other words, *the king*) and, in one, single day, pardoned eleven friends and political allies (those whose cases, in which, William Barr was found to be "intervening"), ranging from convictions for "trying to sell Obama's senate seat, to bribery, and insider trading. Why not? Trump just got away with outright **extortion** and **attempting to obtain foreign interference in an election** – besides, many past presidents have pardoned hundreds of individuals, although, not usually personal friend - and they usually wait until they are on their way out of office.

My feeling is that Trump is just going to make it a normal, now and then, thing, from here on out. He seems to have 'normalized' almost everything that wasn't normal before; "alternative facts"? What the fuck is that, really? *Facts*, the word, itself, is designating that certain things are, in fact, **true**… the alternative to *that*, then, can in no way *also* be true. The last official count, I heard (*and I think it's pretty sad that we've had to resort to hiring someone, who's job it is just to keep track of the President's lies, but…*) Trump has told over 16,000 lies since he has been in office – proven lies – and everyone around him knows it, and they all just act like it's perfectly okay.

He claims he knows more than anyone, even professionals, more than people who are trained for years in a certain field and refutes scientific findings outright! The scientists who are now working endlessly, around the world, trying to develop a vaccine, to save as many of our lives as possible, KNOW WHAT THEY ARE DOING. There is no way Donald J. Trump is smarter than them, and yet, it appears that if Trump announced that the world was really flat, almost half of the people in America would begin to believe it! So, what are we trying to teach our children here? That lying is perfectly okay, because our President does it all the time, now? Why are we accepting this? Why have we accepted it? Have we not yet learned the lesson Trump was obviously meant to teach us??

To Tell the Truth

Trump does act like a child, which is why he is the inspiration of my kids-of-any-age, illustrated book, The Child President. But we are *not* children, so why would we follow one… especially one so blatantly ignorant and vile as this one is? Let us accept the past four years' leadership, *AS A LESSON*, learn from it - and move forward, as better people.

Just imagine how bad it could get; if he were allowed to continue to reign. We have to stop this. Since he was not removed from office by congress after the Impeachment, we MUST take Trump OUT OF OFFICE come November 2020. This is a constitutional crisis; if the president "decides" the judicial system has no authority over him, then what? It isn't hard to imagine the harm that would come, and with this president, it could happen at any time.

Think Long and Hard; Our Future is At Stake

We have toc get the power back from this current executive branch of our government; which forgets he is co-equal with our Congress. Remember, the president is supposed to work FOR US. **He is not supposed to** *rule* **over us.** If all of the above is not enough to frighten every American into voting against this president's continued reign, then as a last resort, I beseech you to consider *his* mental state, and the fact that it is only likely to get worse, and could, at any point, go off the rails.

I'm not one to put blame *solely* on mental illness, as I, myself, live with many of them, coping with several on a day-to-day basis; others on a weekly to monthly basis, but at no time to I ever become a danger to myself or anyone else. Trump, on the other hand, just might. It is my humble opinion that Trump needs to undergo a full psychological exam for mental illness; I think he needs treatment. It is obvious to anyone who knows what it is, Trump is narcissistic, in the very least. I'm guessing he also has some type of borderline personality disorder as well, and probably a very low IQ.

Even Pelosi called his State of the Union speech, February 4, 2020, "his State of His Mind Address"! That made me laugh, but it is also, very frightening when you think about it. We all know it; we all see it. This man tells lies easier than he can tell the truth… his speech, as usual, was full of inaccuracies, purposeful or not. He might really believe the things he is saying half the time. People like that tend to lie to themselves just as easily as they lie to others, so the lie becomes *their truth* as far as they are concerned. Trump will never admit that he has ever told a single lie, yet, the official count *is* over 16,000 times that a lie has spewed from his mouth (or fingertips, on Twitter). We cannot allow this to become the norm for the person we choose to represent our great country in the future.

Our country has been fundamentally changed now, and forever. It is almost as if we are starting over again, states have been reversing women's rights for reproductive choice, bigotry is simply being ignored, hatred is actually being accepted as the norm. ***What have we allowed to happen, America***?

Have we not learned our lesson in the past four years? If not, consider his most recent comments and actions: In an interview with Brian Williams, August 2020, Trump admitted that he may not accept the results of the election, already claiming it to have been 'rigged,' when asked, his response was, "we'll have to wait and see." In August, as well, Trump fired the long-standing Postmaster General and put a friend of his (and campaign contributor) into the position. This person has no postal experience whatsoever and his sole mission was to slow down the delivery of mail, in an attempt to thwart the mail-in voting process because Trump knows, without a doubt, that if every single person in America could submit a vote by mail, he would lose.

The new Postmaster General immediately upon taking the position, removed hundreds of sorting machines from post offices across the nation, and removed dozens of mail drop-boxes from streets in rural locations. This has caused a delay in some essential medications getting to people who need it, and paychecks to individuals who count of the postal service to get their money every month. Congress intervened, quickly calling a hearing and drilling the new Postmaster General, until he agreed to stop making any further changes. They could not get him to promise to put any of the machines or drop-boxes back where they where, however, so Trump succeeded to some extent in his attempt to impede the ability of voters to vote by mail.

Please. We must stop this now. We've come too far, just in my own lifetime, to have fallen so far backward. It's going to take a lot of love, and individual involvement, to fix this. Please think on it, long and hard, meditate, pray (or whatever you do to relax and focus), listen to your heart and your sense of right and wrong. Think carefully before this next election, November (2020) - and however you do it - **participate** in it; and vote your conscience... Thank you.

~Your friend, Dennel B Tyon

Dennel B. Tyon is also the Author of:

A Letter to Heaven (4-part series)
The Child President (a fact-based-fantasy for all ages)
This is The Way I Brush My Teeth
"Spiritual"; A Book of Inspired, Original Poetry
& The Covid-19 Chronicles (Part 1)

Found on Amazon; www.amazon.com/author/dbtyon

(To order direct, go to www.middlegroundpublishing.org
or www.middleground.world or email authdbtyon@gmail.com)

www.ingramcontent.com/pod-product-compliance
Lightning Source LLC
Chambersburg PA
CBHW021339290326
41933CB00038B/981